GW00712332

MEMNOIR

Library of Congress Cataloging-in-Publications Data

Retallack, Joan
    Memnoir / Joan Retallack.
      p. cm.
    ISBN 0-942996-54-2 (acid-free paper)
    I. Title.

  PS3568.E76M46 2004
  811'.54--dc22

                                              2004044771

The Post-Apollo Press
35 Marie Street
Sausalito, California 94965

Cover drawing and book design by Simone Fattal

Printed in the United States of America on acid-free paper.

Joan Retallack

MEMNOIR

THE POST-APOLLO PRESS

By the Same Author

Memnoir, French trans, Omar Berrada, Emmanuel Hocquard, Juliette Valéry, et al., Serie centre international poésie, Marseille: cipM, 2004.

The Poethical Wager, University of California Press, 2003.

Steinzas en médiation. Trans, Jacques Roubaud, Format Américain, 2002.

Mongrelisme: A Difficult Manual for Desperate Times, Paradigm Press, 1999.

How to Do Things with Words, Sun & Moon Classics, 1998.

MUSICAGE : John Cage in Conversation with Joan Retallack, Wesleyan University Press, 1996.

WESTORN CIV CONT'D, AN OPEN BOOK, limited edition artist's book, Pyramid Atlantic, 1996.

Afterrimages, Wesleyan University Press, 1995.

Icarus FFFFFalling, Leave Books, 1994.

Errata 5uite, Edge Books, 1993.

Circumstantial Evidence, S.O.S. Books, 1985.

MEMNOIR

Acknowledgements

Portions of *Memnoir,* some in earlier versions, have appeared in the following: *The Bard Papers, Bombay Gin, Chain, Conjunctions, Washington Square* and the Poetry Project website.

A somewhat different version of the first twenty pages of *Memnoir* was published by Wild Honey Press, Bray County Wicklow, Ireland—January 2002.

My thanks to the editors of these publications.

for Tom Raworth

MEMNOIR

Mem: What's our relation to the past?
Noir: Same as to the future.
Mem: Then what's our relation to the future?
Noir: You don't want to know.
Mem: In other words the jig is up.
Noir: In other words the jig is up.

CURIOSITY AND THE CLAIM TO HAPPINESS

Studies have shown that the brain
prefers unpredictable pleasures.

PRESENT TENSE

it's said that it happens even in nature e.g. during the
childhood the mother might have (had) a taste for film
noir and take(n) the child along

my machine is hooked up to my machin things inaccessible
to the precise methods of e.g. a Brazilian bookmobile
being hijacked in a dark underground garage fiction is
precisely what they now call non-fiction too get a bit too
presonal i.e. Eurydice my dark darling don't worry I can
bear your not looking at me she cri(ed) out i.e. hoping it
(was) true

(now) (here) together in the mix of the modern metropolis
Rio Vienna Paris Tokyo Moscow Hong Kong Lagos New
York Bombay London Mumbai he and she both feel close
to the idealized neuron in the book

some of the diffuse sensations of early childhood may still
surprise us as we consider their names e.g. joy frustration
shame anxiety love rage fear anger wonder curiosity
disgust surprise longing humor pride self-respect fear but
not terror fear but not horror

the mother however might not like surprises e.g. wanting
to know for how many generations a Negro in the
bloodlines can produce a *throwback* the word is memory
the child recalls this use of memory does not know what
to say for a very long time: The soul is inwardness, as
soon as and insofar as it is no longer outwardness; it is
memoria, insofar as it does not lose itself in *curiositas*.

otherwise one could ask at any moment e.g. in what story does an uninvited goddess walk in and roll a golden ball down the hall or why not enjoy the story of lovers in the same vein from different centuries but in the same story from different worlds but in the same story I write down my dreams this is probably not one of them i.e. for a very long time the child want(ed) more than she could say to not want more than she could say i.e. impossible according to any simple formula for mirroring formulas

if e.g. but for the accidental clause the swerve of curiosity
on the monkey bars the flash-bulb memory the wall of fire
outside the window and or something as vague as living in
time i.e. for a time near what seem to be near things swept
into the stream of self-translation in the coincidental flow
of events near disregarded syllables suddenly audible vol up
sudden outburst of song sudden Ha it's too funny how
funny it is to feel sometimes and not others how to
remotely sense a sweet violence in the brevity i.e. the spilt
second glance

> without yards of shimmering adjectives
> description: is description possible can a sunrise
> be described by yards of shimmering adjectives

While the curate was saying this, the lass in boy's clothing stood as if spell-bound, looking first at one and then at another, without moving her lips or saying a word, like a rustic villager who is suddenly shown some curious thing that he has never seen before...she gave a deep sigh and broke her silence at last....Doing her best to restrain her tears, she began the story of her life, in a calm, clear voice.

without the carefully constructed container
story: is story possible: can a life even a portion
of a life be contained in a story: would songs
be better to repair the brain

when if it's curiosity that draws attention to curiosity even
the other animals like us even in nature if for only the
space of time e.g. at the watering hole e.g. during those
times when it's too wide or too narrow for ambiguity the
range of genres might now include humor and but or
horror even (then) there

this voltage through the body is brought on by the senses
senses strictly speaking in logic nothing is accidental the
world divides us into seekers after facts seekers after gold
dig up much earth and find little

or less than a port royal stain it's super being natural not
wishing to symbolize the wish to return to feel as much at
home in e.g. a fortunate sentence as in i.e. an unfortunate
century

some may see at this point which is not an Archimedean
point the necessity to invent a game in which all vowels
are serially replaced with x mxgxcxlly txrnxng prxmxtxrx
txrrxr xntx pxlxtxblx pxst-pxst xrxny xtc.

or that it is not an idle game after all to forgive that they
or we in the slit second of a single pulse to reveal the tear
the tears in all the pages in all their ambiguity paging
through x number of photo albums knowing and not
knowing all that is is not there with only a few clues to
go by e.g. fake cheetah fur fake cowboy hat small dog
straining at leash small notebook or any other kind of book
that can be open and closed at the same time

i.e. all this and more with the ontological thickness of a
scratch and win sheet

look see the red blue yellow green space at the watering
hole hear the animals slurp see the animals roll in the mud
witness the archeological trace of some thing less visible
than a zoological park the mother the father stiff in Sunday
best the insistent curiosity of the child the timing the
timing is all that is off

it is that that is the problem with the timing that it is
always off while it can not be off at all

PRESENT TENSE: CHOICE

e.g. so to not choose the wrong thing to choose nothing
nothing and all given the diversity of forms that even a
soap film or any other minimal surface can at this time at
or on this point that is not e.g. an Archimedean point

or to consider the mother i.e. Archimedea on point to
point out to all how to punch out the holes according to
the instructions that could have (been) the point to
begin with

or e.g. any point that can be made into a world view i.e. a
wild idea the wild idea one has just (had) as a hummingbird
flies by just as one thinks that's a fine deluxe model
bumble bee engine with mechanical wings beating the sky
into a wild idea a hot majestic interlude containing
improbable beauty profanity violence graphic photos of
murder victims all this and more before the clouds part
and the sun turns into a coffee mug or a doughnut

and but though over the years mathematicians have been
able to prove that every noninteresting closed curve is
spanned by at least one smooth minimal surface or surface
reflecting the twisting of the sun into someone's bird's eye
view or the limits of any horizon always being a point of
view just like the one unflooding here

and then the first question on the examination turns out
to be i.e. drymouth #2 pencil poised: What license does
the program of curiosity as the motor of progress of the
sciences give itself and or us? not to say them

and then the child may or may not find that to find one's
position on the graph using xy coordinates one must
reconfigure the geometry of attention in order to comb
the snakes from her hair

PRESENT TENSE: STILL

they would go often to the movies hot majestic interludes
containing profanity violence & graphic photos of murder
victims in black and white interlard(ed) with bitter irony
of if

in this the context of the extreme sport of everyday life it
is necessary to put this in the context of e.g. the extreme
sport of everyday life

or the most extreme object of medical curiosity that one
could hope to hit upon here i.e. the e.g. clarification of the
connections between the way the body moves and feels the
way the mind thinks and feels if one dares to seek these
bonds in the brain of a living animal

or to zoom in on the scene in the darkened room on the
screen the shadow of the murderous aunt is moving across
the screen along the far wall of the screen one can tell it is
the murderous aunt from the feather in the hat and the
dagger in the hand of the silhouette of the shadow on the
wall

or the scene in the neighborhood playground the boy
falling back the boy falling back and back after being (shot)
about to take another bite of his Mars Bar or any other
chocolate treat with a paper or plastic wrapper in the
country where many fear(ed) God & AIDS & Elephants &
Castles & Car Windows & pop goes the weasel on the way
home from school

is it too trivial to ask is this a scale too trivial to ask about
to ask if it is more tragic or more poignant that the child
had hoped to finish i.e. e.g. the candy bar before he (was)
(shot) can the tragic be poignant and vice versa and verso
and recto and the pant cuff gets caught in the spokes and
e.g. the anonymous rider falls off the bike and the optics of
the horizon is questioned on the spot by the Mennonite
Italian who feels his father watch(ed) too many Sinatra
movies and puts too much ham in his omelets

catastrophe theorists say that if we backtrack along the
previous path there will be no catastrophe this time i.e.
not this time

PRESENT TENSED

coming out of the movie theater the world the world is
bright too bright gnomic present tense tensile everything
happening at once the world is full of its own mute history
the fatality of reflection the fatality of nature and culture
the fatality of the German sciences of Kultur the fatality
of i.e. mute history remaining mute the fatality of of the
preposition reaching out to its object even as it e.g. it
slips away

the preceding is much too or not sentimental enough
to accommodate the experience of the child is fatally
wounded i.e. the house is a mess the streets are littered
with trash the lawns are littered with trash the grass is
dying shrubs are pruned to look like gum drops grass is
mown to look like Astroturf replaces the grass up the stairs
of the stoop onto the porch into the house the noise is
incessant the grass is broken the broken glass is littered
with people I have a confession to make I have not
answered my mail my telephone my email my calling my
God my country my conscience my desire to

i.e. what a pleasure to dissolve into the spot on the graph
where the logic of what people are supposed to know
don't want to know don't know enough to have any
opinion on the outcome of another beer belly bakeoff
intersects with the logic of what people are not supposed
to know before or after the crime scene has been cleared
washed down scoured repaired reconstructed renovated
restored rejuvenated retrofitted revenged resettled
unrecalled

also no not also there is memory as in trying to get to the
fire the way to the big light the photon points the way to
itself

PRESENT TENSES

start with a yellow pad a yellow #2 pencil a summer song
an orange rabbit a rare breeze a yellow song a summer
rabbit a zebra finch etc. bring books next time what is it
that you're expecting these circular semantics to say to
run in circles the word exceedingly is interesting here in
these circular ruins this offset press offset print this
sagittal section this dorsal fin this anterior view widening
circumference this widening cross-reference will this
inference make anyone eligible for parole

do you want to say something about that do you want to
say something about that that makes you look smart in
your smart outfit e.g. your Nehru jacket your horny glasses
your upper crust Englicks your queer subaltern view that
is as good as words words words make me a rose

i.e. ergo to stop fooling around in the middle you must
locate three coordinates from which only employees
allowed beyond this point when unexpectedly a wind
might come up and might go unexpectedly away but not
before bringing certain things and taking certain things
away

e.g. quiet little engine beating a pulse across the sky pick
up your #2 pencil write on your yellow pad getting to the
bottom of pot luck there are limits limits to everything but
to refrain from forced propositions is still brave

another example of the way in which a form might not
reflect a purported fact or facts I drop(ped) the tendency
to begin sentences with I long ago she claims anything that
beautiful has got to be evil failure to find an Archimedean
point defined again with nothing larger than a phonebook
found in the debris

this is a method unavailable to the more discursive humanities gee whiz pop gimme a break the book is called *Toward Civilization in America* the story goes that we in America get the fuck out of my space motherfucker can all divide a square into two other squares intuitively given the average city block we don't have to look or sound like the neighborhood or the country we (grew) up in the people we (grew) up with for more than one generation or so we say i.e. this is no Goldbach's conjecture this is no Goldberg variation this is no gold bug this is the story of the good life the end

they call(ed) it a brutal dehumanizing crime once again
a true and tragic story the movie version will be rated
for language sexual situations decapitations &/or less
consequential amputations cruelty to animals the
memories of former surroundings are the scenes of
the most heinous crimes

i.e. ok this is the vocabulary in which you will be locked
up for the next ten years there is no good behavior clause
the study of memory tells us that a person is a place
after all

PRESENT TENSE

e.g. one thing I try not to understand she says is how
gravitation works or from where the force of attraction
comes or the smile the smile in which the body makes this
present felt through one logic or another throughout one
universe or another foot swings out off curb she looks
back exploding into darkest view as letters move across
the line

i.e. she too look(ed) back i.e. there is no past that
point By these fearsome places by this huge void these
vast and silent realms I beg that you unravel the fates of
my Eurydice too quickly run. to say persist and what can
happen will to live by that to hardly know the she the
story tells the consolation in knowing e.g. that early
mathematicians (were) more interest(ed) in example than
proof

screens loaded with blanks bruise blue skies rash sunset
eyes elide gun and index finger she smartly slam(med) the
car door in black and white her high heels click(ed) across
the concrete floor in the underground garage bomb and
rose burst into bloom how to tell the story now without
telling lies you can't you can only leave it alone or
complicate it beyond belief

now during one of those periods when life seems
superficially friendly the more you know the less
indigenous aquiline twilight of the sort that divides
movieland from any e.g. or i.e. that might follow from
this point on

e.g. to love a visceral dichotomy as much as the mountains
we walk and describe as we walk and talk while they are
e.g. roasting grasshoppers and wild boars with tusks
removed on another continent that doesn't come to mind
They called Eurydice. She was new among the shades and
came with steps halting from her wound. this love of
definition leads one to insert any definition here to see it
all and couch it otherwise

i.e. all this is just to slide more easily off the hook to avert
the eyes from or toward the grainy screen to grab e.g. a
yellow pad a yellow #2 pencil a blue summer song an
orange rabbit a rare breeze a yellow song a monarch on a
thistle a summer rabbit a fresh breeze etc. bring all the
books for the course next time what is it that you're
expecting in these circular semantics these circular ruins
this offset sagittal section this widening circumference this
widening cross-reference this crowding of inferences will
anything make her e.g. eligible for parole

it's simply that any body can make its presence felt
instantaneously throughout one universe or another e.g.
(his) foot swings out off curb as (he) looks back (she) looks
back as the realization occurs once the doors are closed
and the lights go down scenes like these can contain
anything at all and more the joys of hopeless love sudden
death violent car chases ambiguous sexual situations
glimpses of strewn entrails war-torn villages ritual rape

among the things I live by she says i.e. along with some-
thing a woman once (said) in a London cab i.e. don't look
back she (said) i.e. they (were) strangers together sharing
a cab i.e. they kiss(ed) their woman's eyes if you don't
know what you want you'll just be used s/he says in the
made-for-tv-movie no more alarming than relatively
tasteful vampire assaults

why refuse entertaining irony dry wry humor display
of imaginative aerodynamics emotional hydraulics fractal
intellectual acrobatics surprising and illuminating
implications drawn over line drawing of mock-up of
monumental prepositional frieze

let's exorcise the crime in the coincidence by turning the
coincidence into a fact (fact) the fact into a symbol (tran-
scendent fact) the symbol into a moral tale (transcendent
symbol) the moral tale into a conjecture in which every
whole number is factored into imaginary numbers thus
avoiding the problem of primes (transcendent moral tale)
or countless other crimes

i.e. the box contained but the squirming matrix of habitual
value-laden self-perpetuating practice (aka can-o-worms)
all but invisible until something dramatic but goes awry is
in fact but the continuous present of and or of either or
experience of e.g. history

she (said) this (was) her favorite line in the movie before it
(was) cut to fast food to the quick not to worry warming
trend continues not alarming warning contains only mild
profanity S&M candy galore and/or difficult subject matter
for children under thirteen

the unnoticed actual condition of the life the erasure of
coincidence the prevention of the crime the irruption of
the coincidence the complete service for eight the
matching sheets and towels the rise of the participles the
unpredicted fall of the prepositions the fully rationalized
forms of alien life the gummy bear erasure the formal
containment of popcorn and coke the sweeping of the
aisles between the shows the vague warnings the trapped
children the brutal surgery the savage war scenes the
sexual assaults the startling profanity the unexpected
violence the graphic photos of murder victims the violent
car crashes the sudden onset of the disease the wounds of
race and class the excruciating paper cuts

is there any way to staunch the flood toward the smarmy
margins I once want(ed) to demonstrate this to be the
case but my margins (were) much too wide to contain
the proof herein is a thought that enters the space left
vacant the figure crossing the vacant lot the ungendered
silhouette intersecting a collector's fact e.g a South
American beetle that glows with so much light you can
read by it in the dark

at any moment another question may arise like an iris
blooming into bloom or the obscene opera buffa this seems
in fact to be

the music swells i.e. the music is swollen with the
sweetness of virtual pain ritual pain the ritual can hardly
contain the virtual pain one thing is for sure one thing is
for certain one aka is standing in for another while the
culprit just (sped) over the horizon spewing technicolor
exhaust

we now know nothing that is not tonic or dominant or
chronic or acute or diachronic or diacritical or synchronic
or diametric or or all or neither except in all the implica-
tions of all the cultural references e.g. in the movie version
there may be sexually suggestive parents an alcoholic uncle
a child trapped in a well laboratory induced schizophrenia
in cute animals incessant gun violence burning crosses
unusual sexual preferences adult language vomiting along
with many respectable binaries good evil male female
nature culture ert inert rapture capture

just finish the damn story and be done with it stop
according to some acceptable convention of stopping

how will one ever get any rest on this restless dangerous
earth far beyond the bounds of deeply held convictions or
questions of making sense

the movie version of this question could contain e.g.
nudity kidnapping rape gay bashing racial epithets incest
ancient grudges vicious murders macabre sexual incidents
sexual situations sexual scenes scenes depicting masturba-
tion gruesome surgery disturbing wartime situations
terrorist bombings conspiracy theories psychosis paranoia
world ruin

the consolations of philosophy are relevant here

PRESENT TENSE

i.e. how to get here by means of a swerve out of the
grammar how it (was) is it that some thing hot dog
happens from Old Norse *happ* meaning luck of the draw
the arrow from one point to the next bring some one or
another to e.g. the point of song i.e. cross-dressed logics
fill the screen on which is playing not a metaphysical
movie but hailed as

they stand in line for tickets and watch(ed) it's vertical
phase fall into and out of ruin this symbolic logic is
the abstract(ed) multivariable calculus of a story that
perpetuates itself only by means of Kummer's unique
factorization or Sophie Germain's primes or Brownian
motion or Cantor dust

PRESENT TENSE

see that shadow on the wall that's you childhood initiates
the child into senses hungers proclivities expectations
exhaustions anxieties terrors horrors humors the
experience of experiencing all that's pointed out and
then the noisy silent rushes telescoping in and out i.e.
stops and starts ruptures and surprises surprise surprise
guess what's inside

this time the instructions read pull out your prize fold and
tear your prize here carefully tear out the red and blue
striped part of your prize place it between your thumb and
index finger gently pinch together to force the prize to
bend let go flick it into a cup flick it to make decisions
who can flick it farther you or your friend take it outside
flick it and watch your prize as it flies out of your hand
into the air

SOURCES

Hans Blumenberg, *The Legitimacy of the Modern Age,* trans. Robert M. Wallace. Cambridge & London: The MIT Press, 1985. (Full sentence on p. 4.)

Miguel de Cervantes Saavedra, *The Ingenious Gentleman Don Quixote de la Mancha, Pt. I.* The Viking Press, New York, 1949. (Full paragraph on p. 7.)

Helen Merrell Lynd, *On Shame and the Search for Identity.* New York: Science Editions, Inc. 1961. (Names of sensations in childhood, p. 4.)

Ovid, *Metamorphoses, V.II., Book X.* Trans. Frank Justus Miller. Cambridge: Harvard University Press, 1958. (Eurydice passages, pp. 25 & 27.)

Tom Phillips, *A Humument: A Treated Victorian Novel.* New York: Thames and Hudson, Third Edition, 1997. ("Words Words Words Make Me A Rose," p. 21.)

James Thomas Stevens, *Combing the Snakes from His Hair.* East Lansing: Michigan State University Press, 2002. (With change of gender on p. 14.)

Note: All "contains" warnings are or are not from *The Washington Post* movie listings.